Gould starts the reader off in the territory of the ordinary before turning a corner into realms of the strange and sublime. Holding forth in a voice marked by brevity and surety she offers poems short on the page but long in perspective: lenses that reflect worlds we thought we knew.

    Margot Farrington, *American Book Review*

Gould educates the senses with subtle inspiration...the beauty of her work lies in its sensitive, uncontrived simplicity.

    Small Press Review

The poetry of Roberta Gould has been described as intense and highly disciplined, concise and communicative with subject matter that varies greatly. Her work should be included in any comprehensive collection of present day poets.

    Choice, American Library Association

The reader will be totally engaged by Gould's poems. They are brimming with fervor and care—for her craft and for our dreaming humanity.

    Vinni Marie D'Ambrosio, Poet. Author *Eliot Possessed*

These are keen witty poems of observation, wisdom and savvy. I enjoy the whimsy-the amazing range and variety and, most of all, the brevity and completeness where she sifts our whole civilization in a mere stanza and gets it right.

    Kate Millett, (*In Houses With Ladders*)

The poetry of Roberta Gould is refreshingly pure...thoughtful and thought provoking through a sense of poetic silence. Nothing superfluous clutters these fine poems. They achieve distillations of experience which is the essence of real poetry and manifest a delicate sensibility at work.

    Daisy Aldan, Poet, Editor, Publisher and Translator

These vital poems strike chords

    X.J. Kennedy, Distinguished American poet

...Gould's poems are an array of evolving presences...a treasury of discovery and self re-acquaintance.

    Donald Phelps, author of *Reading the Funnies*

Roberta Gould is a poet who brings all her senses to her work. ...the focus is beautifully and lovingly on the familiar...poems that are full of spirit and inventiveness.

    Donald Lev, Poet, Editor, Publisher

Woven Lightning
Roberta Gould

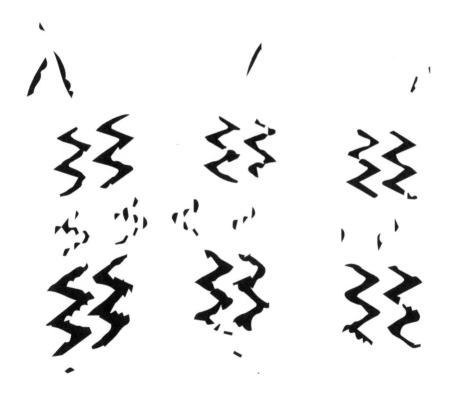

SPUYTEN DUYVIL

New York City

Acknowledgements

Grateful acknowledgement is made to the following publications in which several poems in this volume first appeared:

"About," *Waymark*, 2016
"Another Dog Day," *Like Light: 25 Years Word Thursday Anthology* 2017
"Archeology," *Magnolia Review*, 2017
"Balloon Buddha," *Magnolia Review*, 2017
"Both Ways," *Voices from Here*, 2017
"Floating Off," *Home Planet News*, 2017
"Ghosts," *What History Trammels*, 2011
"Out of Here," *Hudson Valley Transmitter*, 2017
"Seventeen Ropes," *Home Planet News*, 2017
"Spam," *Home Planet News*, 2017
"Stolen," *Loss Lit UK*, 2017
"The Step," *Waymark*, 2017
"Thieves," *Cod Hill Press*, Anthology, 2016
"Too Slow," *Sun Light Press*, 2018
"Victory," *Waymark*, 2016
"Word Craft," *Like Light: 25 Years Word Thursday Anthology*, 2017

My deep gratitude to poet Karen Corinne Herceg for her invaluable assistance and keen perception in helping bring this volume to fruition.

To writer and publisher Tod Thilleman I express my appreciation for his faith in choosing Woven Lightning for publication.

And my thanks to Aurelia Lavallee for her work in Spuyten Duyvil's editorial/ production department.

Library of Congress Cataloging-in-Publication Data

Names: Gould, Roberta, author.
Title: Woven lightning / Roberta Gould.
Description: New York City : Spuyten Duyvil, [2018]
Identifiers: LCCN 2018032719 | ISBN 9781947980693
Classification: LCC PS3557.O894 A6 2018 | DDC 813/.54--dc23
LC record available at https://lccn.loc.gov/2018032719

For Vinni Marie D'Ambrosio

CONTENTS

I.

About

It was a general conversation about finding
and losing, climbing and falling,
dusking and dawning
Yet it was more The air
invisible to us
was replete with creatures
the flies could see
The hands of the clock were no longer there
a flashing and beeping surpassed the centuries
every once in a while

As the river flowed on we didn't step in
watched from a millennial hill
unwilling to keep wheeling along

INTENT

It took the same intensity
as making a bomb
Nothing could stop her on her knees
searching beneath the refrigerator
for the pin that had been swept under
Concentration of a cat!
Persistence of an ant carrying a ton on its back
Is this what one does with a life, someone asked
an hour devoted to finding nothing
valuable?
Just to meet the challenge
fail with awareness
And to stop, ready for the next round of time

STONES

Stones I am holding
spill from my hands
fall to the ground
in their stubborn form
not humble like me
who honors even death

Little do they know
the dust they shall be
when the eons pass
and no one's left talking
Still, I am angry
and kick one down the hill

hasten its change
to pebble to gravel
envying its sureness
I who know it will change
though it seems to defy time,
mute, and stupid

A Definite Type

When ribs are the limit
no breath swells the breast
called "cage we inhabit"

We are the walls
that keep us safe
the narrow halls

and as a river planned through pipe
no longer carving its course
we achieve a definite type

never overflowing the bank
(that ceases to exist)
we're water jailed in a tank

Contained we're confused with our vessel
our systems are sealed
the king is confined to his castle

WHERE WAS IT?

It was in a drawer
the place you hide it
when you don't want to see it
or lose it
in the vastness of life

But wouldn't it be better
to free the furniture of that burden
as it hides what you think
you don't need?

To see it or not
to forget or remember
All's well!
Having or losing
something or nothing
like it or not

There Are No Birds in Last Year's Nest

And the old woman huffed and puffed
up the little staircase
each hour a regimen
filling up the box

I acted as if separate
pretending to see more than I dared to
that I was eternally young,
my deity, Hebe, infusing this body
endless energy surging through me

The distorted mirror cast back
a strange beauty, I smiled
dispensing time with confidence
golden pastilles
ambrosia from Olympus
slow to dissolve
a delight for any tongue

FAME

I have a slow
way of wording
my soul
into shape on the page
  constellated
in galactic alleys
Heavy headed
I heave around
faceless in fuzz
    blur
Would enter
the main run of stars
burst super nova
announcing grandly
    I AM
But distant
past domed glass
its grand convex
I remain ever dim
in sidereal guess

A Birthday Poem on Separation
Dover, England, 1970

They vanish as those differences of heart
all poles in opposition when excluding
we fix upon the safety of a name
that shuts out half the world

Here / There invalid as the split called time
that takes my tears when waiting between decks
and says the tears I see are in my mind,
a figment memory has chanced to fix

would claim as Now the tin tipped steps I place
these feet, you loved, on, say they're truer than
the eyes I see when drawing in my gaze
would place us in two worlds, each with its sun

And now my voice is gone where once I'd come
to fret in wordy futures, I can't talk
How definite the travelers I have been
The whizzing English sky grows slowly dark

until the brimming moon so close comes out
incalculably constant and so bright
Oh peaceful island sky-oh perfect birth!
Oh glass--Ima--that fills with diamond light

SPACE

The bed is wide but I sleep at the edge
A chair beside to extend it

More narrow than a Pullman berth
I ask how I never fall off

Or do I? My dreams break
Open before reaching morning

From a napkin bits of toast
Fall off — yet there's a closet full of plates

And when I type a letter
The sheet prints short

With pen in hand I try again
The letters wend their way to a corner

The sun suddenly appears
I burn bed ink and paper

My fingers catch fire

Three Postcards

I. Before Reading Electra's Vacation Postcard

You will say how the sky is glorious
the light quite perfect
and your heart full I will read your yearly card
It is a thousand years later

I scarcely knew you when last we met
your face, of course, and your voice
which are, perhaps, all that matters
the brother you visit every year
the parents you remember
and that distant acquaintance, me,
who dropped by a few Friday evenings
with so little to say

Should I feel flattered,
that a speck in the cosmos
is singled out as you sit on a rock
near the ocean and remember
what has not faded away?

Do I even have to read you
knowing I served
that you might write lines
fill a half hour and a pretty postcard
one summer afternoon?

You are so faithful
telling me again
about the family house and trips
along the coast you go back to
as you did every summer
speaking as if I lived there then
and were part of the saga
with its zest and rituals

II. After reading Her Postcard

She was on a trip
playing with glitter
imagining the seal was feminine
taking sailing jaunts out to sea
reading and deeply being
herself
Let me imagine I do the same
with never a complaint
a harsh word
a doubt
I dance through a storm
lightning strikes a close tree
It flares and dazzles me
I keep singing

III. Her Sister Penelope Sends Me a Postcard

The picture has a door
we fly through
to join a gliding gull
a boat at full sail
and a sunset skiff
at rest on golden water

The crashing wave in the center
lifts foam to the horizon
reveals impassable rock
making our eyes
the means to freedom

The picture is bliss
and history almost bearable
its static
its barrage

JENNY

They have privatized public information
and I do not know if you are alive or dead
I diddle around for a free way to find you
knowing that nothing is free
holding back the dollars they charge
fearing to know the true reason
nobody answers your phone
I love you
and want to say it
but there may be no one to hear me
and I won't be rejected by the air
that plays its breathing game
going on with or without us
Are you in?
Have you moved to another dwelling?
Did you fall going out?
Did the loss of Jim finally get you?
Or am I late once more?
Or do you lead the way over the river we share?

STOLEN

In the jail of my shoes I began
the long trek home
rutted road with old rain
back bent with time
hauling what had been
fashioned with genius
a shirt with its logo
striped colors concealing
chains linking the oceans

What was I doing that morning
plodding on in illusion
bound for the stolen house
a house no longer there?

Both Ways

I couldn't depict your life
and sell it
so I remained poor
in heart and in purse
I couldn't remember your face
My loss!
So you had to be with me
lest I forget

"What a material being I am!"
unable to hold water in my hands
If I could, there'd be no need
and I wouldn't lose both ways —
wordless, without you
near or far

Sisyphus

Everyday the impossible rock
is pushed up
Cells strain
the sun beats down
or rain
muddies the slope
and cobbles stuck in the middle
block your foot

You struggle
yet there is always
success
joy bursts forth
at the pinnacle
arrival happens
in an instant
you triumph
till the rock starts
to roll down again
smashes you under
unless you jump on
fleet foot
as it gains speed
and dancing balance
as it spins to the bottom

Amazed
you gasp
at what you've saved
You're alive!
but the words are
barely out
when you resume
what you must
grit teeth

brace yourself behind
the igneous mass
and impossibly push
and impossibly push
and impossibly push

Pot/Kettle?

The same restlessness
Uncle would show
visiting a half hour
then having to go
whether for boredom's
or for God's sake

I don't know
not that your eyes seek
another's failing
to look at me
but that you mull
fantasies
anxious to go

Unsettled
like you once
I too chased my tail
seeing emptiness
I tried to fill it

The Emperor In His Clothes
For a most awarded poet, RIP

Are there any creatures
digging through your walls?
Can you eat your toenails?
Do you sink or fall
when any other weather
than the clear of June just past
presents you with the problem
to stay or vanish fast?
Your basic understanding
skewed to whiffs of air,
pressures, currents, passions
to eat, sleep, comb your hair
the days delivered matters:
fish, fowl, to drink, stay dry,
or where to place your money
and how to never cry

Me Me Me Me

I prided myself on my feet
but they gave out
after circling the globe
without resting
Callouses marred their beauty
mine, you see, I am
my body
talking to the mirror

Am I serious?
Well, I know who is acting
and let you in on the secret
My feet!
not the Colossus of Rhodes'
or Ginger Rogers' flashed on the screen
but mine
which I've always prized

The world is getting hotter
There's starving and drowning
but I have an impending pedicure

When it's done
I will kiss my feet

WHO

The one who scratched an eye
and sneezed like me
my twin
out on a beach
where a book
placed us
or
the name of that book
the great one labored to write
from his soundless retreat
  sky
    unending
      and
        we
composite burgeoning blossoms
beneath buzzing humming birds
an open window
and a page
tuning the day

PREPARED

Oh keep it!
The sky's unpredictable
You may need it
You never know!
The black tape across the back
(poor mending)
and your saucer of a hat
that matches
with its little tear near the crown
will stand you good stead
should life take you by surprise
and you're out in the cold, God forbid!
It's a serviceable outfit
and along with your satchel of tricks
you'll be fine
Consider it insurance
no matter what the sky decides
you'll be covered
for sure
Besides, you can rest easy
knowing
I'm jealous
owning no policy
and with just a little kerchief
for my head

WHICH WAY

You woke me up
on an imaginary bus
The velvet cushion you placed
between the backrest before us
and my feet
was enough of a hassle
But you had to describe the process
while doing this
breaking the spell of my traveling solitude

I became very angry and told you
not to talk
which you didn't find endearing
not understanding
where I was where I had been
and the mystery I was bound for

Fully awake now
I took a pink pill
resumed my slumber
knowing you were not to blame
knowing it all was a dream

THE STEP
For Malcom MacNeil

Where it never was
a hollow or hole
crack or split
I don't know
but that you filled it
poured in cement and built it
where I'll enter
and honor you
next visit:
A step!

I never saw the void
that irked you so
I never missed it
on the way to your museum
of the anteroom
in your house
snake skin and drawings
filling the walls
the bow window
looking out on a field
where deer, turkeys and even
a bear appear unexpectedly
as you sit at your desk
and stare or smile
fatigue of work deferred
a moment
the wheel ever turning
labor overtaking thought
Inertia losing

New July

The pain went spinning off
like fleas on unicycles
when awoken
by a mosquito
you awoke me
gazing long
I was clearly
another woman then
Yes
my troubles faded
like gossip, jokes
or just another story
Your face
that new July

II.

WORD CRAFT

The words are dozing
resting from work
at the nuance factory
to regain their original nature
after a lifetime of time and a half

Outside flocks of poets lurk
nets in hand, ready to flick
wrists and capture
the brightest, the starkest, the most subtle,
to compose poems with them,
if life doesn't intervene

If it does, there are always butterflies
and flotillas of clouds drifting by

ARRIVAL

I arched my back
against its forward inclination
like a high diving queen
on a board
I sprang meeting my feet
and rolled like a wheel of flesh
over the land
touching myself
like a snake
time gone
(oroboros)
we the same
mother earth
and this turning
No yesterday
No time at all

Free of my high reach
I was beetle
I was turtle
a simple cardinal
finding seed
This was arrival

No question
This was me

Solstice Light

Every shadow on the road
is a tree in a way
or what you touch
when swinging fences

Your own long body
reaches the mountain
The field is grazed
with the branches' shade

Bliss of emptiness!
The world bursts forth
sliver of bark rising over you
full of the sun

Puzzles

I. Cross Words

Disjointed
on their separate ways
Yanked from the sentence
No longer members of flock
Simply an answer
to somebody's notions
numbered

II. Scanning

I've been searching the room for a superfluous button
puttering about in the first person
scanning the floor though
the sweater can stay open
I'm just setting the morning in motion

Then a porcelain plate slides off the desk
and the dog explores her palate
carefully probing a yam with her tongue
gobbling it down
The two white halves are tossed in the trash
I continue my search
though I note an extra button
the kind knitter imagining this future
sewed on to replace what falls off

Yet the quest goes on
And more time is spent
It's a puzzle-solving mystery
what defines us
not how chromosomes are suppressed
molecules encircling to deactivate them
but this simple persistent scanning of a floor
as the sun shines in

OLD LIFE

I walked a mile to the wind sock
history whirled
ancestors spoke through the mist
By the time I arrived
the weather had changed
By the time I returned
the house had burned down

We kept on
Build again

The wind, at least
didn't whisk us away

ANOTHER DOG DAY, JULY 13

Her tongue extending to the last carton hollow
where eggs cracked, their yokes spilling
out when the bag overturned at the traffic light

This breakfast I discovered the damage
called her from her slumber and coaxed her to lick
the carton, pointing to the little yellow pools

She hesitated then found what I meant
curled her long tongue to every crevice
where the shells had smashed and food lay

I kneeled to watch her tongue do what mine couldn't
lengthening, curling to contain
the surprise nourishment

I stayed down, watched in awe
till all was gone I sang praise then
  And my troubles faded

Longevity: A Scientific Perspective

Decrease your intake like the lab mice
who live longer in their cages
awaiting sparse meals from the Scientist

and are zesty frolicking on calories reduced
turning on foot-propelled ferris wheels
or left to each other breeding on and on

If you treat your mitochondria well
those dear organelles older than us
going easy on food the miracle may occur

Parkinson's not to have the last word
Dementia to stay dormant though you live
more than a hundred as the bible has promised

But whether you have a good sex life
depends on your partner reducing too
unless you're lucky or catch yourself a youth
with no need for your new good habits

BALLOON BUDDHA

The balloon Buddha sitting on the rug
didn't burst but slowly diminished to the floor
Then nothing
freeing the air of its form

There we were both of us
verifying its presence
one receiving it as a sign
the other shrugging it off as a dream

FOR STANLEY NELSON

Wind!
You've saved me from illusion
Just a moment's exhalation
this poem of an afternoon
overwhelmed by your currents
smashes on a rock

Now I can breathe again
disinterestedly
Forget Me Nots on the moss
and a failing tulip
capture my gaze
release it from talking's confusion

and I can contemplate freedom
not the flag but a white butterfly
perched on a fringed yellow petal
its wings pressed together
miming another's eyes
imbibing April's sun

AT THE TULE TREE, MIXTLA, MEXICO

I.

I have come to this tree
To weep for my friends
Who have gone
My vial of tears
Poured to the ground
Near the bird
Who drags its tail
Across the grass
A large grain of corn
In its beak

Nothing
Will ever cut me short
Of the glory and hunger they lived
They who walk here no longer
Names that were love's breath
Thought's lightning
The color of weather

II.

I walk
All my wits are required
To pierce the smudge
Open the horizon

Dystopia

Who freezes breath
icing buds for safe-
keeping in a box
tried to stop the sun
flooding in
with growing light
halfway past the meridian

Who petrified time
sliver of heaven yanked awry
hunger for objects devouring
vision
the sky become stone
wind fierce and birds pinned
flying over no lake

ARCHAEOLOGY

Foraging in the garbage
archaeology of madness
scraps shards and chips
clouds turned to tin
thought become gun
song wanting
And no word
to renew it
impossible

Leave it alone
let it rot as it should

And if you can't dance
don't drag the sky down

INTERVENTIONS

The string bean's in love with the pea
But ardor has cooled and they fight
Good neighbor you want to help

Fear grips your gut and you panic
Is the tiny bride safe?
Should you call the police?

No!
There's a gardener at the gate
You heave a sigh of relief

Mind

From branch to branch
it flings itself
grand acrobat it

can't settle down
The ground rises
meets and sustains it

as no air can
It walks weighty then
crossing the field

pondering how
the hills move

Dusk

In a final dazzle the fence undulates
across the rippled sand of Wheeler Beach

Each slat like a stanchion rises from a shadow
that's the ghost of a whale, this place

And like a light summer sea
the thin range of hazy mountains fades

in a sun still complete that bleaches them out
and blinds us to all but the darkness

Floating Off

The clock in the box floated off
This was a dream *Not To Die*
Tomorrow strode in on stilts
The dead laughed in their gloves

Charred trusses from a fire torn roof
held nests of migrating birds
Boarded windows in the stone walls below
were the start of another life

The sun grew stronger each hour
a bowl full of lilies bloomed
Snails emerged from the dark
The clock in the box floated off

III.

DAWN

Now I will sing
praise for my left hand and all
the flowers that might have been
bodies rotting in fields of rut
and children dead in their cribs

I won't compose commissioned cheer,
hors d'oeuvres never deceived me,
with stipends to reach heights
where mortals go
and a helicopter to prove it

Monster

Was that armored thing,
flat on the ground
in pursuit of my shadow
or feet
just a country creature
or the model for next
year's war,
a machine seeming independent
but killing at master's will?
I don't know
But when it flew off
I remembered
your tale of unknown
monsters and the way
the wired sky kills birds
as we talk and conveniently keep busy
as the absolute mission is prepared
in the filched name of God

ON THE EVE OF THE FALL

They were so far
I screamed with impunity
nothing lost
and a swirl of light over me
not a halo exactly but surely immunity
from what I feared most
the masked men coming
to snatch and devour
with music so beautiful
it seemed to be paradise

And It happened!
All knew now, suffered it
and curse thought they might
nothing changed it

I died.

When they found my note
I was venerated
proof of prophetic powers
I never claimed
what they couldn't fathom
when they'd pass me on the street
my searing words
in a volley of rage
they didn't believe

I Saw Them

After seeing "L'Uomo che Verra" by director Giorgio Diritti

It was another massacre of the innocent
minding their business, living,
they with peasant clothes not neatly pressed
like the Nazis'

who gunned them down near an empty building
and the church, all seven hundred of them,
I knew what they'd do, didn't need another enactment
how the crime would enfold in the filmic telling

It wasn't artistic curiosity that held me
or the wonders of a new language
Bolognese which I barely understood
but the desire not to abandon them

to know and retell it though I knew they were only actors
not the ones who were really murdered
the tots and the infants, the five-year-olds who were crying
the mothers holding them, the panic and screaming

This film is about an infamous event that happened in 1943 that will come to be known as the Marzabotto Massacre, during which more than 770 people were killed in houses, cemeteries and churches. According to the critic Edoardo Becattini, Diritti uses "the language of a community to tell the whole community and the language of cinema to build a message on cultural identity".

What to Do, What to Say?

Tell me why you couldn't become be a gnat
blown through spring's tree by gust or breeze
to buzz on your way with the elements
to annoy us, feed, or simply be the elements?

Why have you chosen to take on the ocean
infinitely filling the boat we are in
before it cracks at a seam
and fills to its limit and we're drowning?

You disappear in the vastness of air
or the depths of endless murk
and can't get out or get back
Could I have helped, I who was born to speak?

Or do I, too, say too little or too much,
wish for nothing or the start or creation?
Am I simply an animal feeding
greedily swallowing everything, Cronus the Titan?

Too Slow

The shell of the egg
was too slow to peel off
as life rushed to hell
rockets exploded with deliveries
to the Moon
and pills filled the belly
of a mulled drink expert
unable to free the avian yoke
hands too clumsy.

Nothing! And more nothing

And then the explosion
And then the long sleep
as if beginning were beginning
snake meeting its tail
circling forever turning
beneath an almost
unending sun

I TRIED

I tried to awaken the dead
and couldn't
and called myself a failure
which was safe closure
It was easy to retreat to the kitchen
feed pleasure seekers
spices from every continent
It was easy to cower in a corner
construct mental worlds that never were
I tried to forget!
I didn't ask why I didn't try again
make the corpses walk straight
see the light
Was I attempting too much
because I had been deluded?
Or was I presumptuous?
I didn't want to embrace them
just to let them be what they never were
so squelched, squashed, damaged, pathetic
stunted and dead of their rage

Spam

Maitlin Pixley
has come into this house
perhaps not a pixie
but apt as they come
I've never seen her
but I'm sending her money
her name so good
it prods my imagination
for longevity or fame
special pills to be dropped
from an invisible helicopter
or a golden ladder
and we'll reach the highest spheres
I don't know
I haven't read her
but I'll take it on faith
and the wizards who got her into my kitchen
Next week, if I befriend her right
she may even start dancing live
in the living room
projected through the earpiece
I wear
to transcend my body
It's the latest
Money's no object
and human progress is
awesome

E-Mail Etc.

Ashley Popplington
writes to me
and a voice recognition robot
reads her fervent message
over the phone
which is my morning
reception of word

I forget what she's said
but I try not to forage
the morass of my mind
to harvest her plenty
for I am clearing out all
but the sky
I will not touch

Still, an ounce of curiosity remains
After all, I'm human

GROWING OLD TOGETHER
For Ray and Richard Chaves, 2007

He bellows curses at the TV
whenever the president leaves his plane
passes the cameras
in his expensive clothes

His wife makes excuses
for his obscenities
when he names the president a fake cowboy
a cracker and a motherfucker

She doesn't like the epithet
nor the explicit descriptions that illustrate it
She was raised to be a lady
though she is not a Republican

The man is 85 and she bears
his anger every day
TV being his main activity
since having the bypass and a pacemaker

They live in the country
What can she do?
When he sees the stakes raised
the country being pillaged

He won't stay quiet, and, shouting,
upsets her, she who
has also had a heart attack
"There's no limit to his gall,

no shame, to his cronies," he screams,
and "They're taking turns with his mother!"
She has no peace at all
and stays with him till the end

Portrait On Montreal Metro

His face was large
square like a carton
beside the thin boned woman
in the new Metro car
His skin shined
and the top of his head reflected
the modern lighting

They were a quiet couple
traveling the city that Sunday
I watched but kept seeing the skull inside him
not different from those in mass graves
or the one in the museum
displaying ancient remains

I didn't cry and I rode the new train
with its many clean windows
and special doors
But though the hard determination
in the man's jaw belied death
I couldn't help fearing his would come like the others'

Whether he considered this I'll never know
getting off a station early
up the stairs forgetting

Out of Here

Get me out of here! My tongue is
burning It's the cactus juice

What do you want from an imbiber?
I didn't pick this lifestyle you know

You with the prosthetic fingernails!
I have to get to the mall

I need to gamble It's calling
Crank one crank 2000 to win

Look! Over the chimney
three bells on the screen tell the story

The man with the dolly moves
his ladder to the shelves for my chips

and astronomers lined at the counter
brandish ads in Day-Glo with pudding

Please give them the ticket the one with my birthday
and tax numbers, my password and wedding ring

Hurry. It's not easy. Did you think life was
a cakewalk? I'll help, too. Are you betting?

On Resuming Reading the Morning Newspaper

I have gotten this far only
to witness old monsters
devour seafarers
olive trees uprooted
flesh burned
and simple minds bought
to praise slavery
with a democratic twist
as dust is dispensed
food stinted
and whips cracked
so that the hand ignores itself
to demolish anything worthy

GHOSTS

Taken by error
their lives return
They are written back
to existence

And their razed house
stands reconstructed
From room to room
they walk

fulfill what
fire aborted
A special ink
has achieved this

BACKGROUND

I used to get up at the crack of dawn
and do a tap dance
On the street the men loaded crates
or emptied garbage barrels
and I'd saunter along
with a song
voicing to the pavement
when no one could hear
I was shy

Sleep is interrupted these days
a cat jumps to my back
eager for attention
The radio never is on
to keep hell out
which filters in when I drive
expecting music
or renouncing it

It's noon and I slough along
as if time were infinite
That's my gift to the god of waste
It's my freedom
I even complain

Meanwhile, over there, I know
starvation proceeds
that killer is king
that nightmare is no longer a word
in the language that it's only background
the wallpaper of existence
where some of us eat

TIRED ONES

The tottering words
reined and whipped
reach the finish line panting
A hullabaloo breaks loose
no hallelujah, no joy
just the magic of money increasing
right side of luck
fortune at the track

Not congealed, not frozen,
fixing the hour, the whim,
nor crystallized with passion
passing through them,
they simply sway
and try to stand on their feet
who once were mountain
earthborn and touching the sky

For the Drowned

Sink if you must but going under keep
your eyes as open as the deep permits
Those creatures want you, watch them eat and know
gifts to be given back are rare and few

Be honored you can calm a raging realm
eager for those in doubt that they exist
The lightning shark, the mythic octopus
starve for your conscious life, take what they will

Humble to the sea as a snail seeking cover
or clouds the cold brings down and the waves break over
May you be their ample fill, now and forever

THIEVES, AN ORAL NIGHTMARE

Why did you steal my teeth
when I only wanted to hear the music?
If my mind wandered
did you have to do your trick
make vanish what I'd lived with all my life?

They were performing a Brahms' sonata
one bowing on spiked heels in a sleek red dress
The other one, pudgy, was ultimate heart
at the nine-foot grand where she sat
Was it then with your sleight of hand
you snatched my mouth's furniture?

And how I wound up on the train after that
I don't know   It was rush hour
the compartments filled
and I was trapped and forgotten in a corner
unable to chew and hungry
soft and unable to fight

They say be grateful that you still have your eyes
Thank god and your stars and try to behave
Complaints are not needed, it's wartime
And keep your mouth shut, without teeth
you're not very pretty

Painting

After an exhibit by Sergio Garval

Don't steal that bishop from the shopping cart
as he's wheeled with a bevy of squatters
in the acrylic river Sergio creates
which is the beginning of water

All are grim in this grayness of time
luxury rampant in its cages
divas devoid of any smile
ready for a new round of business

Then a cloned fuehrer raises a fist
and a goon in beauty-shop helmet trails behind
when a stroke — look up! opens the sky
and dawn glimmers, having taken its sweet, certain time

Was It A Dream?

I kicked the football to the far stands,
first time, without practice
The champion
chose me and I obeyed
took the plastic ball
and exuberantly failed
This after crossing a pitch black boulevard
and successfully avoiding metropolitan traffic
You could call me "Miracle Child"
I was still there

Then I reached
into a wooden barrel
picked the wrong fish
and didn't care
Except the radios were blasting
and money had crossed the wide seas
to buy up the airwaves
And though Beethoven existed
freedom was tied to a post
and the rifles ready
I could bear it no more

Paddling Air

If you say much
you'll lose it
Why grasp it?
Paddling air
pedaling water
smiles fill
your universe

But if the din dwindles
ebbs to a standstill
and silence slaps
your incredulous face
a puddle splashes
your white suit
you'll know courage finally
and next time
may even choose it

VICTORY

They point and poke
but nothing avails
You're cloaked in fog
twirl when they're close
slide away like a cloud
No jabbing finger
can pierce the cover you take
Nothing is there, almost,
and you are nearly a ghost
You chuckle to yourself
inside that insubstantial armor
as they are defeated
mouths agape and darting glances
at your invisibility forced to reconsider it all

WOVEN LIGHTNING

The flaming chopsticks at the fair
are $4.49, if you can
spare a little change
dear tourist
Here's a wren
watch it fly from my ring
Buy a glass hen, Señora
Under a windowed canvas
I stand with my sisters
I've been here ten years
after leaving the dull convention
where I fiddled for keys
lost my glasses
After that I found this place where
plates sing, chains are sundered,
wood is alive and the artifacts
chant with the hours and blood
I drink dusk with eyes open
(after 10,000 deaths and the final tedium)
With what grace their hands
brush dust from cloth
hold hammers high,
offer wares they have made
in the unstated air of great family
If the customers wish
the makers will dispense with prices
work out more natural arrangements
But some buyers are stunted
stare hard for bargains
come with hands in their pockets 70
Meeting takes time
though it seems time has ended
where carved boxes are presented
from which animals leap
and the cloth they have woven with lightning

WHAT I COULDN'T SAY

I never got over spectacular
Wednesday the one following
Trauma six and Tuesday's war
I gave in and stopped counting
In a maze of pseudo eternity
I savored my pastry
Watching the screen flash
Yesterday's history
Mechanical drumming
Beating the day

What's the matter
A few seemed to ask?
I couldn't answer
Guessing they'd hear
What I couldn't say

SEVENTEEN ROPES

Seventeen ropes hang from the sky
A rush to ascend!
The clouds strain but are willing
to hold the aspirers
Yet, three fall to the depths
smash as puzzled dogs watch
content to stare, lick their paws
shake debris from their coats

No one knows exactly where they are going
like sailors, arm over arm, shimmying up masts,
But who can judge the fervor
the passion their pointed aim for the goal?

And it goes on each year
The trapeze is a new diversion
dare devils defy physical limits
their bodies displayed in impossible flight

But the main act
coercing the sky to hold
a display of heavy bodies continues
as they clutch the illusion of ropes
their notion a picture
a mistake
like the air
packaged
but not quite sold.

Roberta Gould is the author of eleven books of poetry. including *Writing Air,* *Written Water, Pacing the Wind, Only Rock, Louder Than Seeds, To The Dogs,* 2016 and an e-book *What History Trammels* (2011).

Her poetry has appeared in Confrontation, Mid American Review, The New York Times, Poetry Now, Catholic Worker, California Quarterly, Jewish Currents, Green Mountain Review, Socialism and Democracy, Helicon Nine, among others. Anthologies in which her poetry has appeared include: *The Art and Craft of Poetry, A Slant of Light, Up the River, Rage Before Pardon, Mixed Voices*—Milkweed Editions. She was also editor and publisher of Light : A Poetry Review.

Gould has read her work widely on public and university radio, Radio Universidad de Guadalajara, Pacifica Radio, WNYC, WKCR, WKCR, at the Pen American Center, the Woodstock Poetry Festival, the Brooklyn Museum and in many libraries. She taught Modern languages for 25 years and has translated the poetry of Sor Juana Inez de la Cruz, Salvador Espriu, Pedro Garfias, Jorge Luis Borges and José Watanabe. An active member of the Haitian People's Support Project and the organizer of a responsible tourism campaign in Mexico, she lives in the Hudson Valley of New York. Her web site is: robertagould.net

CPSIA information can be obtained
at www.ICGtesting.com
Printed in the USA
FSHW011542110319
56142FS

9 781947 980686